HOW THEY LIVED

AN INCA FARMER

MARION MORRISON

Illustrated by
Mark Bergin

ROURKE ENTERPRISES INC.
Vero Beach, Florida 32964

Text © 1988 Rourke Enterprises, Inc.
PO Box 3328, Vero Beach, Florida 32964

Printed in Belgium.

Library of Congress Cataloging-in-Publication Data

Morrison, Marion.
    An Inca farmer/Marion Morrison; illustrated by Mark Bergin.
      p.   cm. – (How they lived)
    Bibliography: p.
    Includes index.
    Summary: Describes the life of a farmer in the Incan Empire in the
days before the arrival of the Spaniards.
    ISBN 0–86592–144–X
    1. Incas – Juvenile literature.   2. Incas – Agriculture – Juvenile
literature.   3. Indians of South America – Andes Region – Agriculture –
– Juvenile literature. [1. Incas.   2. Incas – Agriculture.
3. Indians of South America – Andes Region.]   I. Bergin, Mark,   ill.
II. Title. III. Series: How they lived (Vero Beach, Fla.)
F3429.M846 1988
980′.004′98 – dc19   87–38307
                                                CIP
                                                  AC

CONTENTS

A MOUNTAIN SUNRISE

The Inca farmer sat in the doorway of his small mud-brick home. As dawn broke he gazed across at the distant snow-capped mountains. Soon the sun would warm the mountain slopes and valleys that were so very cold at night. He huddled inside his loosely woven cloak.

Behind him, in the darkness of their home, his wife was preparing food for the day. A hot stew, some corn and a drink of *chicha*. When it was ready he and his son would leave to work in the fields. First he had to let out the animals, a few llamas and sheep that spent the night in an

Right *The Inca empire stretched far along the Andes mountains on the west coast of South America.*

enclosure near to the house. During the day his little daughter would tend the sheep. The menfolk faced the tougher work tilling and planting on the stony ground of the high mountain slopes.

As he rose to go, the peasant saw the huge black form of a condor circling in the sky. He was happy to see the bird because the farmers believed it brought them good luck. Collecting his wooden tools, the father called to his son and they set off together, in good time to start work in the emperor's fields.

The farmer and his family were members of the Inca empire, a civilization that successfully survived in the Andes mountains of South America from about AD1200 until it was conquered in 1532 by the Spaniards.

THE LAND OF THE INCAS

The Incas began as a small group of people living near the present-day city of Cuzco in Peru. During the thirteenth and fourteenth centuries they became the strongest of the local tribes. Then in 1438 their most famous ruler, Emperor Pachacuti, came to power. With his son, Topa Inca, he conquered most of the other tribes living in the Andes. By the time Topa Inca died in 1493, the Inca empire stretched 2,000 miles (about 3,000 kms) through the mountains and along the Pacific coast of South America.

The Incas called their land Tahuantinsuyu. The word means "the land of four quarters" because this was the way the empire was divided up. Each quarter was divided into provinces. The emperor, who the people believed was descended from the Sun god, ruled supreme. He governed the empire with the help of Inca nobles and officials who were appointed as provincial governors, leaders of the army and priests. The nobles enjoyed special privileges, like wearing very fine clothes and having several wives, and in particular, paying no taxes.

Right *The emperor ruled over his people with the help of nobles.*

Below *The snow never melts on top of some of the highest mountains in the Andes of South America.*

6

THE PEASANTS

It was the ordinary people in the empire who paid taxes. As taxpayers they were organized into groups of 100 and were in the charge of a local chief or noble called the *Curaca*. Tax was not paid in money, as this was unknown to the Incas, but with produce and in work done. In this way the ordinary people supplied everything that was needed for the emperor, the nobles and the priests. In addition, each taxpayer was expected to spend some time on public duties, such as building roads or working in the mines and also serving in the army.

The farmers worked hard. Their homes were high up in the Andes, where the land was difficult to work and the climate sometimes very harsh. But because the Inca empire was well organized, the peasants knew their position in society and the work they were expected to do. They lived with their families and friends in communities called *ayllus*, where they felt secure. There was always enough food for everyone, and the state would look after anyone who was sick, handicapped or old. There were many happy festivals to enjoy, with plenty of music, dancing and special food and drink.

There was, however, very little opportunity for a peasant to change his way of life. Just occasionally a clever boy or beautiful girl might be chosen to serve a member of the nobility, or even the emperor, but most children were brought up to help the family and work on the land.

A government official uses a quipu *to count the number of sacks of food the peasants have brought for the emperor, nobles and priests.*

GETTING MARRIED

This silver llama may well have been a wedding present given to a wealthy Inca noble.

Children stayed at home until they married. Most people were expected to marry, and were obliged to take their husband or wife from their own *ayllu*. Girls were usually 16 or older, while the men were normally married before they were 25. If a girl or boy could not find a suitable partner, then a marriage would be arranged for them by a government official who regularly visited the villages. If, on the other hand, more than one young man wanted to marry the same girl, the government official would sort out that problem too.

The marriage ceremony was performed by the local *Curaca*, in front of the family and relatives. Gifts were given to the bride and groom, and the couple were lectured by their parents on how to lead a contented married life. Then the wedding party could begin.

It was the responsibility of the community to provide a house for the newly married couple, and relatives gave presents that would be useful in the home. The couple were also given land that they could farm for their own needs. For the first year they were not expected to pay taxes; it was more important for them to settle comfortably into their home and to start a family.

Wedding gifts were often household items. This wooden drinking mug was probably a gift to a couple.

11

A FARMER'S HOUSE

Very few trees grow in the Andean highlands and there is little wood for building, except on the warmer, wetter slopes. Stone, which is still quite plentiful, was reserved mainly for building the emperor's palaces and the houses of the nobility. Most of the ordinary peasant homes were built with adobe mud bricks and thatched roofs made of a tough local grass that is called *ichu*. The Quechua and Aymara Indians of the Andes still use *ichu* and adobe bricks for building their homes today.

The farmer's home was small, with one low doorway and often without windows. Because it is so cold at night in the highlands, the peasants needed to keep their huts as warm as possible. There were no chimneys, and inside it was always smoky from the clay or stone stove on which the food was cooked. The peasant farmers used clay cooking pots, with kitchen tools made of

The Aymara Indians still use adobe mud bricks and ichu *grass to build their homes.*

12

A government inspector would come around to check that the peasant women kept their homes clean and tidy.

wood, bone or copper. They ate on pottery dishes and drank from wooden or pottery mugs.

Furniture was scarce. They had no tables or chairs as we know them, just an occasional adobe brick bench. Instead of a bed, the peasants wrapped themselves in blankets on the dirt floor, and usually the whole family slept together. Any spare food or clothing was kept in simple clay pots, as even with so few possessions, the peasant women were expected to keep their homes clean and tidy. So much so, that government inspectors regularly visited to check on them.

13

FAMILY LIFE

A young married couple looked forward to having many children, who were brought up to be tough. One writer, who knew the Inca people and wrote about them, said that the babies were always washed in cold water and often exposed to the night air and dew. Their arms were bound inside swaddling clothes for more than three months and they were kept all the time in their cradles. Mothers did not take babies into their arms nor on their laps, as they believed this would make them "crybabies."

There were no schools, and children did not learn to read or write. This was because the Incas had no written language and so had no books. Government officials, though, did use a device called a *quipu* for keeping records. It was made of colored strings with knots representing numbers and information. Only a few trained men understood the *quipus*.

At the about the age of 14, boys and girls prepared to become adults. They were given new names and new clothing. For the boys, this included their first loincloth, which was a sign that they had reached manhood. Then the families celebrated with music and dancing.

This drawing shows an Inca official using a quipu.

Right *The Incas thought that it was good to put babies outside at night to breathe the cold air.*

DRESS AND WEAVING

Peasant dress was practical and simple. In addition to the loincloth, the farmer wore a knee-length tunic, sewn together at the sides with holes for the head and arms. This was sometimes decorated with geometric patterns. Over the tunic he wore a large cloak that could be tied on the shoulder to leave one arm free. The farmer's wife wore an ankle-length sleeveless dress, pinned at the shoulder and with a sash. She, too, wore a cloak, sometimes fastened with a large decorative metal pin called a *tupu*. Hairstyles differed from one region to another, but women wore their hair long and often in braids. Both men and women wore sandals made of untanned leather, which they took off in wet weather, as the soles softened in water.

Most Inca clothes were made of the wool of the llama and alpaca, domesticated animals native to the high Andes. But cotton was grown on the coast and was used in the warmer, lower valleys. The peasant families made their own garments, the women

Left *The wool for the peasant's warmer clothes came from the llama and alpaca. Lighter clothes were made of cotton grown in the valleys.*

Weaving on a loom. The loom is tied to a tree and strapped around the woman's back.

spinning or weaving on wooden looms at all times during the day. Ordinary cloth was in natural colors such as browns and cream, but brightly colored vegetable dyes from native plants were used for special clothing. It was the job of young girls to search for the right plants.

17

WORKING ON THE LAND

Land throughout the empire was divided into three parts. These were not always equally divided, but in every region one part belonged to the gods, one part to the emperor and the remaining part to the community. Inca farmers were responsible for cultivating all three. Supervisors were appointed to look after the harvest of the lands of the emperor and the gods, and the boundaries of these fields were very carefully marked. The lands belonging to the gods were always cultivated first, and the crops provided food and offerings for the priests. Produce from the emperor's fields was kept in government store houses for distribution to the nobility, the army, or to those who could not farm their own lands.

Water was transported to the fields along channels.

Every year the community lands were redivided among the peasants by the *Curaca*, who made sure each family had enough for its needs. In this way the *Curaca* could arrange for part of the land to lie fallow. He was also responsible for organizing a fair system of water distribution. This was important on the steep-sided mountain slopes, where the Incas built agricultural terraces that were irrigated by carefully made water channels.

Inca farmers had only simple tools made of wood, though they might occasionally be tipped with bronze. The most important were the foot plow and the clod-breaker, both used for breaking up the ground, and a hoe for lighter work.

The farmers had to grow crops for the emperor and the priests, as well as for themselves.

FOOD AND DRINK

This beautiful wooden water jug has been painted with a very detailed Inca design.

for making the drink called *chicha*. The farmers drank *chicha* every day, but especially at festivals.

The Incas ate twice a day. Food was always boiled or roasted. The peasants liked to eat vegetable soups and stews. They spiced them with peppers and herbs, which were also grown on the lower slopes and made the food tastier. The only regular source of meat came from the few guinea pigs, which the peasants kept in their homes.

A wooden Inca drinking pot, shaped like a jaguar's head.

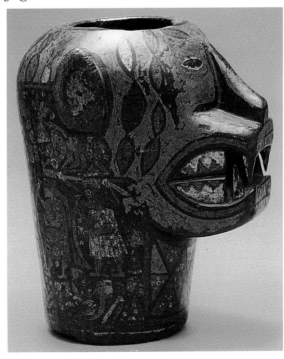

The crop most widely grown by Inca farmers in the highlands was the native potato. It was particularly valuable because the farmers could preserve it by a form of freeze-drying: they exposed the potato to the sun during the day, and then to the freezing night. It this way, the potato dried out and could be kept for several months. Another hardy plant, the native *quinoa*, which is rich in protein, was used in stews. Corn, or maize, which is quickly killed by severe night frost, was grown more successfully on the lower mountain slopes, and was especially important

FESTIVALS AND GODS

The beginning of the Inca farming year was in August and it was celebrated with a great festival. Farmers and their wives chanted as they turned the soil, digging in fertilizers of llama dung and guano (bird droppings) in preparation for the sowing season in September. The Inca

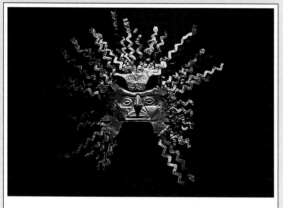

A gold mask of the Inca Sun god.

farmers used names like "growing time" and "time of heat" to describe their seasons. They were particularly anxious waiting for the rainy season to begin in December. The priests of the Sun god fasted, and sometimes, if the rains were late, black llamas were tied up, without food and water, in the hope that the Thunder god would hear their sad cry.

Once the rains arrived, they usually lasted until April. The main work then was weeding and protecting the crops from scavenging foxes and birds. Festivals were held almost every month, with offerings to the gods. The farmers grew more anxious as the time for harvest approached. Sometimes they dressed up as "guardians of the fields" in foxskins

and with slings, to frighten away anyone who might damage the crops. The women would often watch over the fields with a small drum. Once the harvest was safely gathered in, everyone joined in the greatest ceremony of the year, the *Inti Raymi* Festival of the Sun. They would dance to the music of flutes and drums, and make sacrifices in honor of the gods.

Besides Viracocha, the creator god, the Sun, which protected and ripened the crops, was the most important Inca god. Other gods included the Moon and the Stars, though the Andean farmers specially worshiped the Goddess Pachamama, Mother Earth, because she would look after the soil.

The festival for the Sun god.

CRIME AND PUNISHMENT

The Incas had a fair though strict system of law. If peasants obeyed the rules, the state looked after them. If they did not, they were severely punished. They were discouraged from stealing by not being allowed to own luxury goods. But crimes against the government, like burning down bridges, were taken very seriously. A farmer found to be stealing from the fields of the emperor could expect to receive the death sentence. This was done in various ways: by stoning, hanging by the feet, throwing from a cliff or beating the head in with a club.

On the other hand, a person found stealing food when they were in real need might be let off with just a warning. Or if a murder was committed in self-defense, there were several other possible forms of punishment. For the Inca peasant these included torture, exile and the *hiwaya*. The *hiwaya* meant dropping a large, heavy stone from a height of about three feet onto a man's back, which might kill him. For the very serious crime of treason, there was the much-feared prison in Cuzco, an underground cave filled with poisonous snakes and fierce animals.

GVAMBOCHACA

The keeper of the bridges checked them for safety and prevented them from being damaged by anyone.

Right *For very serious crimes against the Incas' rulers, prisoners were sent to this dreaded cave.*

24

CARING FOR THE OLD AND SICK

An Inca farmer stopped work when he was about 50, or earlier if he was not fit to do the hard work. The government would find him alternative, lighter work, and he would no longer have to do his share of tax work. As he grew older, he still had to help in the house and with the young children. In the Inca empire no one was allowed to be idle, and even people who were handicapped, such as blind and deaf people, were expected to work and pay taxes.

People were excused from work only for the time that they were ill. The Incas believed all illness was caused by evil spirits and so they sought cures in magical and religious practices. Some so-called medicine doctors used herbs, of which there were many on the lower mountain slopes, but they were very secretive about their medicines. The Incas did not suffer from many of the diseases that we have today. Illnesses like small pox, measles and scarlet fever only arrived later, with the Spanish conquerors.

Left *The Incas were skilled surgeons. They were able to perform operations on the brain, by cutting a hole in the skull.*

Dolls made of cotton and reeds were given magical significance and buried in Inca graves.

When people died, they were buried with the tools of their trade. The relatives dressed in black, sang and danced to mournful music and for many years afterward respected the memory of the dead person by making offerings of food and *chicha* to the gods.

27

THE MITA

A farmer spent about five years of his working life doing the *mita*. This was a form of tax by which men worked in the mines, served in the army or joined the public work force. While the husband was away, his wife carried out his farming duties.

In the Inca empire there were mines of gold, silver, tin and copper. Objects and ornaments made of gold and silver were valued very highly and could only be used by the emperor and his nobles or to honor the gods. Only married men worked in the mines, so that their wives could provide them with food. If a man became sick, he was allowed to return home at once.

The Inca army was well organized and well fed from the government store houses. From the time of Emperor Pachacuti in 1438, it was

Peasants were called into the army as part of the mita.

involved in many campaigns. In the army a peasant had the chance to prove his ability as a soldier, and in return for outstanding service could win for himself and his family some special privileges, such as a few luxuries in the home.

The public work force was employed in the construction of buildings and roads wherever they were needed. So a peasant farmer might find himself building an

emperor's palace in Cuzco or at work on one of the excellent roads that reached to every corner of the empire. The Incas were skilled craftsmen, and their magnificent buildings of massive stone blocks that fitted together perfectly without mortar are still standing today.

The mita *was a form of tax. Men had to spend five years doing work for the state. During this time the women carried on working on their farms.*

THE EMPIRE ENDS

Unfortunately for the Incas, rumors of their gold and silver spread to Europe. In the 1500s explorers arrived in South America. They were anxious to make fortunes for themselves and their kings. In 1532 the Spanish soldier Francisco Pizarro landed with a small band of men on the coast of the Inca empire, in present-day Peru.

Spurred on by stories of incredible wealth, the soldiers endured a terrible journey across the mountains to the town of Cajamarca, where they found the Inca emperor, Atahuallpa.

Atahuallpa welcomed the foreigners, believing them to bring him good fortune. But Pizarro deceived Atahuallpa. They executed him and conquered the magnificent Inca empire. Many Incas fled and hid high in the mountains. The ruins of Machu Picchu, one of the last Inca strongholds, can still be seen today. This Lost City was rediscovered in 1911 and remains a monument to the Inca people.

The remains of Machu Picchu, which was an Inca city hidden high up in the mountains of Peru.

GLOSSARY

Adobe Bricks made of mud dried in the sun.

Ayllu An Inca community, somewhat like a village.

Chicha A kind of beer made from corn.

Curaca The local Inca chief or noble in charge of a group of about 100 peasants.

Fallow Plowed land that is not used for growing anything for a year.

Guardians People who take care of or guard something or someone.

Geometric patterns Pattern shapes of mathematical origin, creating regular designs.

Hiwaya An Inca punishment; a large stone would be dropped on a prisoner's back.

Ichu A grass used for thatching houses.

Irrigate To supply water to land by building artificial ditches, to help crops grow.

Mita Public duties done by peasants for the good of the country, such as building roads or serving in the army.

Mortar A mixture used to hold bricks together.

Nobility Members of the ruling class, such as the emperor and his family.

Protein A substance in food that is vital for the growth and health of people.

Provinces Different areas of a country.

Quinoa A cereal plant used by the Incas to make stews.

Quipa A device of colored strings and knots representing numbers and information, used by Inca government officials.

Swaddling clothes Long strips of cloth wrapped tightly around babies to keep them warm.

Taxes Charges made by a government to provide for the running of the country.

MORE BOOKS TO READ

Atahuallpa and the Incas, Marion Morrison (Franklin Watts, 1986)

The Inca, Patricia McKissack (Children's Press, 1985)

The Incas, Anne Millard (Franklin Watts, 1980)

The Incas, Barbara L. Beck (Franklin Watts, 1983)

Indians of the Andes, Marion Morrison (Rourke, 1987)

INDEX

Picture acknowledgments
The pictures in this book were supplied by Marion and Tony Morrison, South American Pictures. The map on page 5 is by Bill Donohoe.